Something
in the Air

Something in the Air

Tom Clark

SHEARSMAN BOOKS LTD.
2010

First published in the United Kingdom in 2010 by
Shearsman Books Ltd
58 Velwell Road
Exeter EX4 4LD

www.shearsman.com

ISBN 978-1-84861-108-5
First Edition

Copyright © Tom Clark 2010.

The right of Tom Clark to be identified as the author of this work
has been asserted by him in accordance with the Copyrights,
Designs and Patents Act of 1988. All rights reserved.

Cover photo: *Something in the Air*,
copyright © 2010 by Cristina Bozzoli
Book Design: George Mattingly at GMD, Berkeley, California

Some of these poems first appeared in *The Argotist*,
House Organ, *Jacket* and *The Poetry Project Newsletter*.

"After Wang Wei," "5 P.M.," "January," "September," and
"Pink Trees" first appeared as Viking Dog Press broadsides.

"A free market wonder...," "Aqualung," "Blur / Lens," "Club Sahara,"
"De Ira Dei," "Moira, or Fate," "Single," "What Is That Bright Star Next to the
Moon Tonight" and "'Who needs Apollo...' *(with Ted Berrigan)*"
first appeared in *Single*, a Longhouse foldout.

Contents

Something in the Air • 1
Blur / Lens • 2
Multiple Screen Window Display • 3
To A Certain Friend • 4
Expansion • 5
Every Day • 6
Little Cantos • 9
Whistle Buoy • 11
In the Dark Mountains, Brilliant • 12
Eldora • 13
Sequoias • 14
Dreams of the Blue Morpho • 15
Beautiful Thing • 17
Collection • 18
Up the Creek • 20
Momentary Visitor • 21
Hope • 22
Musing • 23
Lecture • 24
Aporia • 25
Nights at Sea • 26
"This diminishing of things…" • 27
Sweet Peas • 28
Walking Out • 29
Solarity • 30
One Morning in December • 31

The Riddle • 33
View • 34
Greed • 35
Ideology • 36
"A free market wonder…" • 37
"Meant to be…" • 38
Paradiso Terrestre • 39
Small Change • 41
Single • 42
Loop • 43
Bliss • 44
The Movies as Natural History • 46
An Unnoticeable Star • 47
Postconceptualism • 49
1968 • 50
"Walked into state…" • 51
Aqualung • 52
September • 53
January • 54
All Souls • 55
Elephant Cemetery • 56
Ancestors • 57
Thinking About George • 58
Scenes Along the Road • 59
Where Is the House of My Friend? • 60
The Shadows • 62
Origin of the Speechless • 63
The X of the Unknown • 64
Talk Gets Old • 65
Comic Interpretation • 66
The Lake • 67
Club Sahara • 68
Three Easy Pieces • 69

Twisted • 71
Sedge • 72
The Pharaohs Sacrifice Themselves
	Before Her • 73
Time • 74
Moira, or Fate • 75
"A point is fixed…" • 76
"In this river…" • 77
"Because they are desiring…" • 78
Meditation • 79
Tunnel • 80
Palafito • 81
Motion, 1953 • 82
5 P.M. • 83
Pink Trees • 84
Blue Spring • 85
After Wang Wei • 86
The Nightingale • 87
Keats on Shipboard, September 1820 • 88
Hans Bellmer • 89
Friedrich's Dream • 90
Caspar David Friedrich and the Interior
	Dictation of Landscape • 91
Heaven Up Here • 93
Witnesses • 95
The Practice of Painting • 96
An Echo of Time • 97
Slow Life (for Joseph Cornell) • 98
Southern Cross (to Giuseppe Ungaretti) • 99
"Who needs Apollo…"
	(with Ted Berrigan) • 102
What Is That Bright Star Next to the Moon
	Tonight? • 103

Andromeda • 104
De Ira Dei • 105
Anyone There? • 106
Crepuscular • 107
White Moon • 108
Survey Research • 109
Contraction • 110
Glassitude • 111
Entertainment Medium • 112
The Self-Unseeing • 113
Mnemonic • 114

Something in the Air:
    statement on the poems • 115
Biographical note: Tom Clark • 116
Poetry Books by Tom Clark • 117

Something in the Air

The identity sign
held Wittgenstein
is a lie

Some kind of
dust or
pollen in the air,

falling,

a light cloud
drifting
earthward —

"I"'s blurred
memorial
dispersing into

several
unsorted
particulates

Blur/Lens

The "I" and the eye
A glass for seeing
Always cloudy
The days go by
The world spins round
The subject is always moving
The mind can't keep up
It's all a blur
The eye and the "I"
A glass for seeing
Always cloudy

Every two hours I wipe off my glasses

Multiple Screen Window Display

Like so many tiny pixie tv's
Flashing messages to each other all night
The hundred billion neurons in your brain
Replace identity as such with deep
Cosmic gossip while your body's arrested
in mid flight back toward an old savannah —
A hundred billion neurons seeking shelter,
Losing that deep self because you're asleep,
Lost in your dreams, a functional state
Of your brain lapsing into disappearance,
Your brain not bothering to compute you,
Your sense of who you are going up in smoke,
Though if the soul be several not one
There's only now and that now has presence.

To A Certain Friend

Presence comes before everything, even before being
The you to whom everything once belonged
If by everything one means the fullness of nature's beauty
You must remember now that much has been taken from you
Grief too will go from you as from sorrowing songs
Sorrow goes, leaving nothing for you after a while
But the memory of the melody, some old familiar tune
That's lingered on long past the moment you first sailed
Gracefully into the room, as if all the modern languages
Were coming down to me so that I could say these things

Expansion

Distribution of moments.
Memory. Attention. Expectation.
A light plane, a feathery piano
Solo. The time of everyone
In the world comes apart
In pieces, a slow quiet
Dispersal. The poppies are still
Furled into themselves
Chilled morning maidens
But the musky red antique
Geranium droops open as
Do some purple blue
Unnamables whose scroll
Unravels backward like Arabic.

Every Day

Grammar tells us
what kind of an object
anything is. So does light.

"Thought
is surrounded
by a halo…"

You can feel yourself thinking
but can you think yourself feeling?

A state of what?

"You're a smarty pants
do you want to dance?"

Touch is important
in a dark universe,
but print is useless
much less unreal

Mechanical Tao

The robot pushes small obstacles out of the
way, goes around heavy ones, and avoids slopes.

The BIG crayon
for little fingers

Where is it written
that we must write
right side up?

Advantage —
ah, it stays with us
past the asking

Are we
some kind
of filter, some
diode
it's all being
run through?

I am here with this (my mind, etc.)
"I am not here with my mind"

Learning to forget
occurring in the instant,
uneasily wise
& so, poorly aware
Space isn't
in Language —
or as the child cries
"Outside! Outside!"

I walk in
on occasion

One room fronts on
open, unqualified spaces.
The other is bound
by a wall. All its
area is thought up.

mind
lines

Around
nouns
people are
nervous,
possessive

People on television
give you their
public self
like people
on elevators

"What has the greatest importance
is not the twelve tones, but,
much more, the serial conception…"

More hair
Every
Day

Little Cantos

1

orange harmonies
bubbles resonant open
literal yarn beans electricity
chatter angels

people
atrophy dream
tears leafy eddying
faraway buzz
planes above
jets

seashell
membrane

starlight octaves
oscillating breakfast
hemoglobin
woodchuck

Strawberry
Nymph
throne

2

garden starfield food
bugs

thermostat trick indigo
white universe

cirrus slabs zone benzene
parachute
verbena
library
chronometry
Nahuatl
bumblebee

sunfish mesas
shampoo
diatoms fly

purple
phonemes
yellow-orange
bobbin corona newspaper song

Whistle Buoy

That grey droning note
I've heard every dusk

Neither owl nor foghorn
But similar to both

The low fluted "day-is-done"
Of some unknown warbler

Atonally breathy memo
Of universal mysterioso

Tucks misty roses away
In the dark's soft envelope

Safe under a lion's paw
Of starry numerology

Whose silver figures
Flecked by receding surf

Otherwise float unfathomed
Into the liquid night air

In the Dark Mountains, Brilliant

Nature says be cool, nothing ever mattered
More than spending a smooth eternity
Watching this punk purple martin splash
In a trout pool of the Sierra Nevada

Before dying, being released from time
And becoming the feather glance light
Surrendered in these deep blue wing vibrations
Flashing against the grayish matte air

Of the lower ponderosa and blue oak forests

Eldora

a valley
of aspens
and wild flowers

with the wind
dithering in them

Sequoias

High over my head
and
long after I'm gone

Older and
wiser and
prettier by far

Closer to God
knows
what future

Dreams of the Blue Morpho

1 *Instars*

The larval bower swells with passing instars
A swarming of wings in the air of the swimming dream
A mothwing fur grows over the dreamer
Let us call him Mister Dim the Image Collecting Man
Who dreams the dream of the Blue Morpho
And feels his soul being changed again
When soundlessly the pupa on flimsy wings
Emerges from the tree line just before dark

2 *What the Blue Morpho Does in Mister Dim's Dream*

Changes shape

Puts an end to sleep
by quick shimmerings
of its wings
on his eyelids

Moves toward a silent estuary
where a pure world of alpha states
forms into a delta
an island on stilts in the night
in the dry tropic rains

And then in the end
the Blue Morpho Menelaus
and the Blue Morpho Peleides
mate

3 Now It Starts

Around dinner time
the pupa hatches
emerging from the trees
on flimsy wings
just before dark
(twilight comes early)

And this is the beginning

4 In Time

Spring sunshine
irradiates the stunted jack pine
with kingfisher light. Time sleeps

for the Blue Morpho. The wink
of wings as she probes
the orange-throated corollas

of shaded woodland flowers
was programmed eons ago

but as she spirals up, thinking
to break away on the airflow —
here comes
the guy with the net

Beautiful Thing

Beautiful thing in the evening I remember you
I run my hands through your fur
With its thick passages of blue gentian
And deep black emerging from snow
And forget the pain
That remains of the shattered body

It does not surprise me men in the night are searching for you
Twenty thousand nights I've searched for you
I see their blue eyes turn to fire flies in the dirty oaks
As the night vehicles go by
The grinding of a clutch
Laboring uphill in the terror corridor

There's a strong electric light on a pole
And out of the night comes you
O beautiful thing
Someone is searching for you in the night
On all fours
He crawls toward you

This is the news
This is the memory of your crepuscular mothfur touch

Collection

Specimen must not be wetted,
too sharp a point can mutilate
A rush of intaken breath

attends
the pinning of the specimen
a nervous flutter

of wings at dusk —
a certain risk in trying
to wrest away

the net transparent
tough and light, yet
she slips through —

too wide spaces in the naming?
A film of language, then
that won't crush the wings?

Transparent
speech, bobbinet
locked mesh —

where are
the air dancers
tonight?

Locked in?
Silk or nylon
can be torn, and the ripping

sound of great wings breaking
free *lasts* —
in this moment

now
which is why
killing bottles are a must —

Wide mouth tube with chopped
up rubber band lips,
pinch if you must

but use
potassium hydrochloride
for clutching her with taxonomy,

and liquid carbon tetrachloride
for holding her there
in an image, *close* —

these are the collecting toxins —

Up the Creek

Had been trying to find its course for years
sans mechanical intervention
toward some thought somebody had had about something

but on the way kept getting lost in the tall weeds
and forgetting its purpose must have been
to arrive somewhere not to stay to splash

Momentary Visitor

Momentary wary sniffing visitor
Remote unmanaged ancient mystery
Flickers in your revenant amber gaze,
Prowling the pharoah's dusty gardens
For prey gone a thousand years, still time goes by
More slowly in the space from which you appear.
Egypt is no longer, this makes you watchful
In the changing light beneath the light foliage.
And clouds come over those great soulful windows,
Your portals on this clouded stranger world.
If you could speak to us, what would you say?
My name is Time Wanderer, I come from far
Away and remember none of what's happened to
Bring me this distance to look in your young eyes.

Hope

The happiness promised in names like Lord's
Valley and Wind Gap recedes like the fading
Of a rainbow, yet hope walks in anyway,
Where there's life she's there — nature's utopian
Possibility remains part of the scheme
As long as there's a breeze to blow the past away.

Musing

I didn't know the tune of the lyric book you were reading sadly
It was someone's pensive elsewhere song
Its words had never reached me
I didn't know whether you were absorbed in your reading
Or merely thinking about something else

Lecture

Elsewhere perhaps life was going on, the business of the world was being done, connections between individuals were being made, troths plighted, who knew, maybe even babies born.

The person speaking droned on.

In the third row someone yawned. A notetaker paused and glanced toward the window. Outside it was a bright spring day. Oxygen, carbon dioxide and sunshine conspired to produce undeniable evidence of natural process in the form of chlorophyll. The red end of the light spectrum having been largely banished from the atmosphere, a blueness perhaps reflecting some great water-mass prevailed in the patches of sky visible through the branches, across which also passed every now and then a lazy, buttery cloud. An oblivious bird tweeted on the other side of the glass. Time almost stood still.

Elsewhere perhaps life was going on…

Aporia

"I am at no loss for information about you and your family," said Demosthenes, "but I am at a loss where to begin. Shall I relate how your father Tromes was a slave in the house of Elpias, who kept an elementary school near the Temple of Theseus, and how he wore shackles on his legs and a timber collar round his neck? or how your mother practised daylight nuptials in an outhouse next door to Heros the bone-setter, and so brought you up to act in tableaux vivants and to excel in minor parts on the stage?"

There had never been any need to be unkind.

And so the days went by, and then the nights, and the wig bubbles drifted.

Doubtful coves with a heavy plundered cargo but only an empty heart to hold it in, not copper stripped, and subject to the worm.

Bewilderment and embarrassment make poor allies in a storm.

The sounds of the old argument come out of the past to haunt, and then like a briefly recollected passage of music are lost again, released into the grey slipstream of unretrieved memories, to flow back to wherever it is that everything that's ever been forgotten is stored.

We tuned in then to the Shipping Forecast. From Finisterre, intermittent rain, visibility one mile, and rising slowly. Dover, visibility ten meters, and falling rapidly. Spindrift vision, a minute twitch of the imagination. A state of puzzlement, as the Captain felt looking into the fog.

Nights at Sea

> *One half of the world cannot understand*
> *the pleasures of the other* — Jane Austen

Once again, that eternal conversation
Going on in the the dark across
A short suspension bridge between ships
That may as well be island worlds

Of unknowing ones who understand
Each other, perhaps, better than they do
Themselves. As if understanding helped.
And now, as the obscure harbor looms,
Not exactly a port safe from the storm,

Explosive words mine the dire straits;
We ask ourselves, how can we navigate
These narrows without deceiving beacons
Flashing come off it and give us a break
To misguide us?

"This diminishing of things..."

This diminishing of things, as if
Sleep were a miniaturist working
In the darkness, to the dimensions
Of a mini-theatre echo-chamber
Through which stray air currents dragged their ghosts:
A point of light appearing in the dream,
A glimmer almost swallowed by the room's
Dark corners at first, grown in a little while
To the restless thought sleep's escaped again.
The thought cast its anxious reflex into
The dream, and I awakened then, castaway,
Drenched in the sunshaded stones of afternoon.

Sweet Peas

The sweet peas, pale diapers
Of pink
And purple
And powder
Blue, are flags
Of a water color
Republic
In which morning
Is being born
Again

Walking Out

Early morning light archery
Moon pictures propped on the dawn gestalt
A plum violet flood of light
As I walked out into it once again

Solarity

A shower of gold on the wave
Wings make
A black hole
Opens in the sky
And clarity comes through
Like water from a hose
Call it daybreak

One Morning in December

No end to Thinking
Dreams are ghosts in disguise
Awake the mind's hopeless so
At a quarter to six I rise
Run 2 or 3 miles in
The pristine air of a dark
And windy winter morning

A light rain falling
And no sound but the pad
Of my sneakers on the asphalt
And the calls of the owls in
The cypress trees on Mesa Road

The macrocosm is still
Pre-dawn traffic all but nonexistent
Until
A VW goes by with surf board sticking
Up through the roof like a shark fin

A girl on a black horse says "Hi!"

And then the sky clears
Large yellow full moon appears
Sets over my shoulder
As I run home from Palo Marin
In the pre-dawn coldness
Blowing small white
Airpuffs out ahead of me

On my right the ocean shines
To the east a Rose
Of Sharon saffron-ness sweeps
Over Mount Tam whose
Sleeping volumes are still
Snow-dusted

And slowly
Overhead the whole bowl
Of sky brightens and expands
Counter-clockwise

When I get back you're
Sleeping with your hands
Between your legs as if praying

And your hair blown back
Across the pillow like a mane

The Riddle

When the answer
Cannot be put into words

The question
Cannot be put into words

The riddle does not exist
So it's good morrow

As day's lovely banner unfurls
In the world

Blue dawn suffused
With red and gold

Before the dogs
And birds awake

I walk with beauty
Like the night

Down the dark cliff
To the murmuring sea

On the path to enlightenment
And inner peace

With one black eye
And a bloody lip

View

Apocalyptic thinking presumes
All this has never happened before

And will never happen again. I know,
Before the morning's eyes have opened,

The apocalyptic view of the world
Supposes things do not repeat themselves.

But they do. And they do. And they do.
The sky clouds up. A new storm comes on.

Whatever is going to happen next
Moves forward to complicate the view,

So that it is impossible to miss
All this will never happen again, too.

Greed

Slinky-toy history: life coils itself
Slowly, and then uncoils, descending the stairs
Defensive reaction by defensive
Reaction. We thought we were only here to please,

Yet as in that old painting of the peasants' feast
The banqueter represents the destroyer.
Eating is not only feeding oneself,
It is digging one's teeth into something.

Ideology

Ideology dates back to the veldt,
Blood in the dust, the lion's rage against
The antelope it's about to have for lunch.
For the luckless prey prayer's all that's left,
No ideology's yet been known to incorporate
Mercy as a feature. But of course all this is irony.
No lion's yet been known to subscribe to a noble lie.

"A free market wonder..."

…their having stumbled into
a free market wonder

land in which value
had come to seem forever

detached from even the
thought of actual labor,

there grew among the young
men on the street

an assumption that
they could do anything…

"Meant to be..."

Meant to be
a propaganda image
for the "war effort"—
the four of
them together
beneath the low
one room
school house roof—
meant to be
collective incentive—
understood now
as an enhanced
past. Yet can't help half
imagining half
remembering
the original:
all that
direct open
American
certainty of life,
all that
awkward earnestness,
all the best
laid plans, all
the good intentions
in the world.

Paradiso Terrestre

We have always been here
it was always ours

words not as signs but powers
of suggestion

this is paradise
in the present tense

no seconds no
minutes no hours

no distance between
object and expression

what is seen or heard
felt in the same moment

by the one who sees and the one
who is seen

the one who speaks
and the hearer of the word

all creatures bound
by a kinship persisting

until appeared
the middle managers

and thus began
history

the vision thickened
the speech grew slurred

and awkward
and everything stopped

Small Change

Sense life's
expense of spirit
in a waste of shame's
oh maybe fifteen cents

and can't spare it —
ah lighten up, it happens
without spending experience
value doesn't apply

Single

The world not
the abuser, the
poor single
thing inside
the person's skin
not the
abused. And
yet, and
yet.

Loop

The ego is
perfectly
able
to become aware
of the chance
it has
to leave
the realm
of self
preservation
behind
but this
ability
alone
does not
suffice
to realize
that chance
and what
you get
instead
is just
what happens
night
after night

Bliss

Hello, where are you, and who?
Will we find bliss together?
Will we reach out in the night and touch hands across the inky
    gulf of eternity?
Or will it merely be tangled wires and short circuits?
A configuration of transmission cables and silicon chips?
A string of zeros and ones comprising a locale? A line of text
    simulating a human being?

Will the wisp of hair that clings to your temple and which you
    brush away distractedly with one hand
While you gaze into the lighted box before you, become a
    silent chord in the song we make together?
Will your mountains and islands and deserts be forever hidden
    in endless clouds and fogs?
Will the clarity of retouched screen-saver bliss never envelop us?
Will we dwell forever in the sock puppet lie of identities we
    believe we have chosen in order to make contact?
Will the sleeping husband in the next room rise and walk
    across the universe to speak to the sleeping wife?
Will the lover of a thousand dreams find a voice on another
    continent?
Will the isolated universes of our separate beings remain on
    parallel tracks to infinity?
Will we die before we have learned each other's real names?
Are our names so important after all?
Is there a "you" that is more than an assemblage of
    reconfigurable selves bundled together by accident?
An offscreen individual who is not simply a phantom or a ghost?

Will our dreams propel us into a future
We have before now only projected or vaguely imagined but
    never thought we'd actually see
In which the limitations of gravity which once pinned our
    bodies to the earth
Are left behind like vessels in a suddenly landlocked harbour
And the knowledge of certain death which heretofore
    obsessed us
Is forgotten in the flowing forward motion of a new and not yet
    explicable Spirit of Ecstasy?

Hello my friend I'm just one more window in you
Wherever you are
Whatever you are
Said the one billionth self as always infinitely fluid
To the no one
In the flickering lights in the modem

In the ethernet where you are what you pretend to be
It's surface surface everywhere
And no one is there
But you
And you
And you

The Movies as Natural History

What is it that freezes us into the frame like this?
Petrifies objects wherein life's congealed
Secrets lie like sleeping beauty preparing
For the awakening of the living moment's kiss?

The blood camellia blooming vivid in the syringe
To dissolve with blue heaven in a white cloud
Which as his thumb depresses the plunger
Roars like a train wreck into Vincent's arm;

The still-life aura — natura morte — that lights up
The compact numinous Czech M-61
With huge silencer which Butch now espies
On the kitchen counter, just as, setting down

The milk carton, he drops two Pop Tarts
In the toaster; the rabbit trapped in cabbage patch look
Frozen on Vincent's vacant kisser, as, surprise
Melting into sudden understanding, he enters the kitchen.

An Unnoticeable Star

Particulate matter
sucked within the event horizon
dragging space and time
into the ergosphere
whole galaxies never to be seen again
after one sardonic Ray Milland grin

The universe is not a friendly place
to grow up in

Just another pretty face
but behind that blank
and vapid mask
a supercilious nonchalance
with just a faint
undercurrent of malice

A safecracker hiding his
whiskey bottles in the chandelier

Something disturbing
yet horribly true about
his mixture of extreme
irritation and disbelief
with almost gentlemanly disgust

Cosmic dust and gas
spiralling into a black hole
at the center of a galaxy

Something about reality
Ray Milland couldn't stand

Postconceptualism

I like breathing better than wireless ideation
But strange is the human meat
When it is ripped out of the sky
And arrows are shot into it

Nothing is personal then
And everything is true
Including love's great circumambience
And the skull in the mirror

The mortal intimation
Of souls of beings long since lost
In a forgotten past
And the deep pink nescience

Of the thought evacuated tissue
Glaring back at you
Through the empty eyeholes
In the mask

1968

All the while I was
being numbered and
stored by history
as an example
of something
as flat and thin
as a picture
in a textbook
or an image
on film
I remained under
the illusion I was
merely living

"Walked into state..."

Walked into state
office building
in flat white
light of cold overcast that,
without sun,
makes all days
seem alike — boat adrift on
ocean sans shore
floats aimless
on endless waves
falling and
again lifting.

Aqualung

Slow cling of gray white rain at oyster dawn
As if thin cloth were being continually torn
Inside outside, soft sizzle of wet rubber
Hugging four lanes of blacktop traffic back
Firing bridgeward over this slicing sluiceway
That cuts slick and gleaming as a blade
Through dull wool light leaking from blue pleura

The locked in aqualung silence of what?

September

Walking in the woods, I found the thread
of dread that led to the endarkened
clearing — as a flame
fibrillates in the leaves
around the edges of the trees
into which one fears to go — so courses through one
a thread
of light that flickers —
the factum
is the fatum —
9/22 AUTUMN BEGINS (7:05 P.M., EDT)
as evening falls

January

Hélas! My narcissi are stinky
after only two weeks: 2:52 a.m.
twenty one is it? degrees on the mercury ball
a serious shivering within the spiritual timbers
in the town named after the bishop
who argued away the existence of the material
why then doth it weigh so
(contra the hypostasis of the individual)
upon us all

All Souls

The moon coming through the curtains
makes geometrical patterns in bars
a calligraphic grid through which pass
the ever vigilant ones
the souls of "my" dead though of
course they're no one's
not even their own any more merely
messengers of the mirror negative
dispatched from a mute past
to efface a haunted present

Elephant Cemetery

To feel a sense of loss is our next assignment. We zoom in on an elephant graveyard. The red baked earth of the plains, the dry, withered foliage. The great beasts are taking turns paying last respects, pawing with heavy gravity maybe just to stir up a little ceremonial dust. A kind of halting inquiry, tentatively caressing the remains of the loved one with a tenderly lingering trunk. Gentleness perhaps masks the quality of interrogation in this process. Ah, dear gone one, what do you know now, is there any of it you can tell us?

Ancestors

1946 suddenly
to remember how it
was to walk into the
kitchen of one's now
dead ancestors and see the
brown gold or porous
sepia light falling
ground reels under
that fleeting sense
of how the world will
feel in this place long
time from now, when
remembered by no one

Thinking About George

for George Schneeman 1934 – 2009

Thinking about George in
January in California
The sinking sun lights a few late
Streamers of cloud with faint blooms
Like the distant inklings of
All one remembers

Under the bare plum tree
A white cat sleeps on a chair
And squirrels chitter in the ivy
Audible for once in the vacuum
Created by traffic's absence
All one remembers

Returns in a moment and
George is present in the mind
And we are alive in the light moving
Into the darkness of all that is lost
To fill the emptiness of the day with
All one remembers

Scenes Along the Road
for Arthur Okamura 1932 – 2009

Thanks to you, Arthur Okamura
for ping pong and vibrating cows
& now THAT, too,
is past
& petering out
"behind" us
like bus stations
in that Simon & Garfunkel
song, something about America?

Windy, a day of candid shots (clear eyed)
of long ago
distant handsome guys, who are they
what do they do for a living?

We decide to ride in the car
along the road, why not, to where
soft people, hardly stars
finger the proofs of a
beautiful first edition, high
in the artist's studio, with
the pleased poet standing by.

Where Is the House of My Friend?

In the false-dawn twilight
a rider enquired of a passer-by:
Where is the house of my friend?
The sky paused
The passer-by held a branch of light
which brushed the dark sand

He pointed to an aspen:
before you reach that tree
turn off at the garden path
that leads into a space more green
than any god could dream
and go down that path
as far as the wings of honesty can reach

Continue beyond the end
of the first part of your life
and then turn again
take two steps
toward a flower that grows alone
at the foot of the fountain
of the story of the earth
stop and you will be swallowed up
by fear transparent as water

In the closeness of the space that flows
something rustles
in one of the surrounding pines
a child has climbed up
to pluck a young bird

from a nest made of light
and you call out to that child

Where is the house of my friend?

(after Sorab Sepehri)

The Shadows

There's many a good tune played on an old fiddle
Said Samuel Butler to his shadow

The shadows of old men in entirely different centuries
Go ever with me now

Origin of the Speechless

Inconstant and strong
Unsettled and wandering
Impossible to control

Irresolute, fickle
Willful and restless
Wavering in purpose

Whimsical, capricious
A curious mimic
Never exhausted

A good deal of thoughtless
Swinging through the trees
Followed by

An even longer era of
Somewhat ruefully
Thinking It Over

The X of the Unknown

Sweet notes in dimensionless clusters
Eighth notes and fluttering cue balls
And Tibetan gongs in the side pockets
Those are what Charley Johnson heard
When he got his bell rung

He could stand but he could not see
He could hear but he could not talk
He could think but he could not walk
And over his head in the thought balloon
Little birds tweeted

So he continued to stand there
Until they came out and got him
And even then it was hard to lead him off
For he seemed like a man leaving his mind behind him
Somewhere there on the ground

Talk Gets Old

We have to do the best we can
That is our sacred human responsibility
Said Einstein to the gorilla
Who yawned and smiled patiently once again

Comic Interpretation

This isn't one of those old funnybooks
Where Popeye & Co. keep on coming back
To live their lives exactly the same way
Over and over again, sans apparent
Reasoning behind the idiotic
Reiteration of the rhyme, which,
Like life itself, tender plasmic issue,
Concession to nature's force majeure,
Comes squashed between doughy, juicy buns
Constantly headed into that gaping
Maw sunken into the kisser of Wimpy,
Is it?

The Lake

The silence of eternity
Is like organized crime
It spreads its roots everywhere
In these lacustrine retreats

We inhabit Goodbye, Lake
Poets! The radio is chinking out
Caprice Espagnole by Lao-Tree
Its cold tinkling magic echoes across the peaks

Lake Life I want to take a bath
In you and forget death
Waits at the muddy bottom
Although I live in the tree

Of poetry and sing I have no
Water wings
And fear death by drowning
In a mirror image

Club Sahara

At the oasis: dusk, dark intimations,
Faint simoon. Marooned Cassandra, waiting.
Consciousness: wily nets, loosening strings.
Odor of sex. Arpeggio-like oud
Runs up and down stepping-stone vertebrae.
Recumbent Traveller, in halter top,
Consuming some lilac-colored fruit. Moving
Without thought, without knowledge of anything
Into life, as ice melts in the mountains,
As the blue desert moves into a dune,
Lifting its yellow tresses, sifting, rushing
Over amber sands to a horizon from
Which night flings up a giant sky, billowing,
Weighed down by tons and tons of mute stars.

Three Easy Pieces

The Anarchist

When it got dark, a girl began to sing. She sang in Russian, and, with the wind sighing in the trees as accompaniment, it sounded very sad. A chill crept up the lawn from the lake, where a mist had started to rise off the water, creating green, blue and red halos around the lanterns of the piers. Across the lake, lights danced in the windows of the big estates. Stars gleamed overhead, notes on the musical score of the dark. When the wind went through the trees it made a sound like the strumming of a vast harp. Suddenly the girl stopped singing. The night crouched on all fours, poised to spring; then a clear peal of laughter rang out.

Core Sample

The continuing overtaxing pressure to adjust to the administrative world leaves people no time to do anything but bore into the material clay of their lives, as though their destiny had been to evolve into drill bits, boring deeper and deeper, moving vertically downward forever, indexing, storing, scooping out new digital data, the important questions met along the way drowned out by the roar of the earthworms.

Cheating

One wants to be able to reach out without looking and touch death on the shoulder; but when one's hands encounter something cold and hard in the alien dark, like a touch of the marble statue's arm, with bits of loam still clinging to it, one draws back, realizing this is not the way.

Twisted

Psyche asks why love's so dark
after making love to the river
all night long
as if she understood the wind and the rain

•

There where no language ever yet was known
to read across Time's face
from right to left the Chinese conception of fate

•

Loss of soul control coordinates (guidance systems)

•

The continuous twistings of threads
on the night of the soothsaying dream
wherein no business is done no lies are told

•

"Nobody can know everything" he said
"not even the best of the diviners"

•

The tortured *memoria*

•

Even the most beautiful parachutes
travel away from heaven as they move through the sky

Sedge

Lorelei with wet hair riverine,
black delta, white beaches
coming out of her moonlight shower —
her cold, cold beauty is the chimerical
other for whom the subject's
erotic longing is like a phantom itch
in a part of the body that died long, long
before we started to patrol this part of the river.
Dark eyes, and wet hair trailing in
the reeds like a subjective language of sedge
through which the timeless current snakes.

The Pharaohs Sacrifice Themselves Before Her

Time is the sweet cheat that unhinged
The Egyptians. The fugitive object
Of desire keeps fleeing, the symbol
Denoting speed in physics must now
Precede any expression of her value.
Algebra of desire yields to total
Calculus of need: instant nothingness
In which there flows an invisible current.
When it flows through the tomb, one is forced
To bow down and worship an obscure,
Mysterious and implacable goddess.

Time

2500 years Before Proust
Xerxes overthrew the stalwart
Lacedaemonians at Thermopylae.
He built a bridge of boats, allowed
His anima her autonomy and
His prow to be cut through by her armada,
Carving out a dark continent of desire
To identify with the object's body
That lasted 2500 years.
Through her nothingness there flowed
An invisible current. He sacrificed
Himself before her in an effort to
Recapture all the points of space she had
Ever occupied. It was vain — and when he took to
Thrashing the sea of events with rods
In an absurd attempt to punish
The engulfing of his treasure
Fate lost patience with his act,
His fleet was destroyed at Salamis
The same year he pillaged Athens.

Moira, or Fate

A flash of the spinning hand of Moira at the head
Of the bed upon which bolts crackle and strike,
A flash of the hand of nature in the genetic chain,
Divine anger signifying energy, law
Destiny of all men being the same, death

One doesn't argue with this any more,
Amid the blasted neurons, than a bell with its flaw:
The crack of determination under the hood
Of the chromosome. Her messages get lost in the soft
Blue dust left by the memory of light.

"A point is fixed…"

A point is fixed at the
intersection between the
personal and the rest

of the cosmos, and that
nexus is the source
of the flood of speech

the desperate polyphony
of conflicting meanings
empties continually into,

all signs condensed into
a single line leading
out from this dust mote sized

fraction of the history of
a very tiny star into the
silence everywhere around it

"In this river…"

In the eerie phosphorous
green light that needles down

in the middle of the dream
she sleeps with mouth wide open

as if to gasp or cry out
a black sun is rocked

In this river of stars and exile
longing rage apartness sorrow

love and hate light streams
through space tearing open a mouth

"Because they are desiring…"

Because they are desiring,
desirable, mortal, and

death-bearing, persons must,
like in manic 50s

tv gameshow gauntlet,
flee in and out of uncanny

state of strangeness, changing
direction compulsively as

drives are triggered and fade
according to readout of

current surge lapsing
back again into inertia,

momentum sustained
as positive charge that

sparks up red shocks, pulsing
across the calm grey green

display window in constantly
shifting systolic waves

Meditation

The clock at the bedside, mutilated like all things today, in these times, had no hands, only bright red numbers, which went on displaying themselves all night, one after another, 3:48, 3:49 and so on, as long as there was electric power. Usually there was. Often he wondered what it would be like to be blind. Life would go on in the dark just the same except for the numbers, they would cease to exist.

Tunnel

Does any of the meaning you think at times you see
Disappearing ahead of you just out of your reach at the
    tunnel's end
Actually materialize once you're gone (no longer looking)
And was it ever here…? After the end of all the stories you're
    left with
What?

Palafito

This habitual convergence of images half waking
Dawn returns to the ancestral village
Where a house on stilts is raised
As by elongated legs of water birds
Up above the surface of the lagoon
The noiseless slap of oars is soft and cool

Motion, 1953

And they came into the New World.

It was 1953. The name of the tune was Motion.

The reeds were hard and soft at the same time.

At sunset beyond the bows of the beached ships the streamertails were flashing.

They resembled blue and green trick semaphores, light signals rising and flaring against a seaward deepblack glory.

Rita Hayworth and Stan Getz were dancing in a West Coast airplane shack made of thin porous wood, everything looked laminated, aerodynamic, in the painted hangar.

Takeoff into conflicted breezes, moving through a baffle of bamboo, gangway rolling slightly.

The ghost of a change happens to you if you let it.

Swaying bodies come apart, tropic clouds race a paper moon, a hot wind, paper palms falling down.

Some fragile coral green undersea thing is haunted by your breathing, the gardenia of your mouth, the jasmine of your skin, the fragrance of Negril, spices cast upon the night to fathom the remembered impulse of your inner life.

5 P.M.

A seam opens
in the traffic
flow I
hear this
mockingbird in my
backyard
and when it's gone
Satie
played by
Shearing
on an antique FM
drifting
down through yellow plum
leaves
against the blue rush
hour sky

Pink Trees

The message erupts each springtime
What we do know we don't know till we know it
Has slipped away through the airy spring branches
To drift up in thin grains through the gray-white sky
And here on the blue clay earth below it
Down a yellow Spanish East Bay hillside flow
The pink trees.

Blue Spring

The blue spring wind drifted the plum boughs up to the sun, an offering. In that moment you were one with the universe, even if five months gone from it, suggested the cricket song. A mourning dove cooed into the blue-powdered white thought. A set of wind chimes gently dinged somewhere not too far off. The alert brown alleycat's ears twitched like anxious pans, fanning the air to pick up and sort out the confusing soundmix the wind carried. Somewhere, very faintly, briefly in the distance, when in an instant of mercy traffic and all the other racket stopped, a tinny radio signal grew rich with shoals of orderly baroque violins.

After Wang Wei

Chilling down by the water
stopped to watch clouds drift
clouds drift clouds drift
bumped into mr. green
talked laughed forgot
it was time to go

The Nightingale

It was dark in the covert. From the unseen underwoods came a trill. My friend who had taken me walking in this green Somerset lane paused to listen.

Calm-throated, then rising, a quick buoyant spiral of notes, keen, sweetly piercing. A few seconds and it was over.

"Have you ever heard a nightingale?" my friend asked. This was May 1965 or so.

I hadn't. I was, what, twenty-four, twenty-five?

In the spring of 1819 Keats was twenty-three. He had not far to go.

Coleridge also heard the nightingale in Highgate, early, that forward spring.

The reclusive night-wandering bird, pulled toward the poets' gardens beneath a waxing moon.

Sorrows, mysteries, businesses and sillinesses: human things played out to the backdrop of a deeply earth-tuned melody.

And then, forever, the brevity of the northern summer nights.

Keats on Shipboard, September 1820

Twilight, a few white clouds about and a few stars blinking
The sweet signals that guide me to this unknowingness,
The waters ebbing and the Horizon a Mystery,
Sea surface calm and strange fish circling below in green

And violet shadows at the turning of the tide,
A sense of a kind of quiet submarine growth
Of darkness in the deeper, outer channels,
With my last English evening coming on.

Hans Bellmer

Why does Bellmer's
art express so well
the fallenness of men
their living under this spell
as if out of each one
had come another
who walks beside that one
and bears that one's name
but feels nothing

Friedrich's Dream

Caspar David Friedrich's
technique of gathering
empty pastures of light
saturated with a kind
of melancholy radiation
on the middle of his canvases
came to him in a dream

When he worked
at painting a sky
no one was permitted
to enter his studio
because he believed
God was present

Caspar David Friedrich
and the Interior Dictation of Landscape

He avoided Goethe's invitations to come to Weimar and work
    together on a collaboration
He was too busy collaborating with certain beings
inside him
whose commands he found so much more compelling
they came alive
during his solitary strolls into the countryside at dawn or just
    after moonrise
his favorite time
during which he often paused to sketch
a group of trees a cloud a boulder a row of dunes or a tuft of
    grass
at their urging
Every true work of art (he wrote) is conceived in a sacred hour
and born
from an inner impulse of the heart

As he grew older depression distanced him more
and more
from the world of men
I have to be
on my own
and I have to know I am on my own
so that I can give myself up to what is around me
he wrote
in declining an invitation to tour the Alps
with a Russian poet
who admired his paintings
I have to unite with my clouds and rocks

I have to unite with everything around me
in order to be what I am

When the mineral world dissolves into the cosmic flux
the animal and vegetable worlds will have been long gone
but the beings who existed inside Friedrich and dictated his
    landscapes
will still be carving vast silences out of elemental gulfs

He had a special interest in the moon
He used to say
that if after death men were transported to another place
then he would prefer one less terrestrial than lunar
in order to allow the beings inside him to feel at home

Heaven Up Here

Beyond nostalgia
And expectation all life
A process
Of removal from life
Translation

Into whatever's out there
Or isn't
Air or aether
Entering celestial clouds
In the moment of liftoff

A light feathery moment
In which
To depart is to arrive

Violet shadows glow
As if filled with nutrient
Of the afterlife

Blue avenues of ozone
Blank atonal diffused
Through the reflected square
Of sunlight
On the floor beyond the waiting
Room chair

Wouldn't it be nice
Like leaving the room
Without leaving your chair

Though I haven't yet been convinced
I'll be so gently
Hurled
Into that floating world

Witnesses

He was, however, impersonal, not in his method only, as all great artists have to be, but he was what would be commonly called impassive, that is to say, unemotional, in his conceptions as well. He loved impersonality, the absence of expressed emotions, as a quality in things.
—Bernard Berenson, *Italian Painters of the Renaissance*, 1897

These Piero
della Francesca angels
have choirboys'
soft ephebic faces
yet seem eternally detached
and unmoved
in their attention
to what unfolds before them
the faint
hint of a smile
of thoughtful contemplation
curls the edges
of their oval mouths
they take in the mystery
with steady eyes
and no fear
of error or trickery
as if they could
simply by witnessing it
make the world a radiant place

The Practice of Painting

Morning beckons from the phthalocyanine shade
Heaviness sheds its weight
There's water everywhere

Unrivaled dawns and dusks so wild

Hands like leaves
Move chastely in the air
And many little cries — according to Alberti —
Come out of the branches
Near by, whispering foglie...

The wax paper crackles around the sandwich
In Botticelli's hands
As he relaxes beside his canvas
Having lunch
Amidst
The Madonna
Of the Magnificat

An Echo of Time

It is only mourning
For the mind's
Lost moment
That has
Preserved
Like an echo of time
In these rustlings from the past
A touch of fabric
Of metal
Or of wood
A presence
The living moment
Continues to miss

The power of time
Imposes itself
In the materiality
Of the objects
And textures

This infinitely specific
World which
Also
Will begin to decay
The moment
We look away

Slow Life (for Joseph Cornell)

1

Cinematic blossoming of blue planet minutiae
Giuditta Pasta
Slow life

2

Blue windows behind the stars
And silver flashes moving across them
Like spotlights at movie premieres
Long cool windshield wiper bars

3

Can one make works that are
Not "of" art?
Fresh Widow / French window
Painted light blue
With black leather "panes" so that
At the life opera
All day it's night

4

The butterfly gently opens itself like a fist
Dividing into wings and drifting off
Over the cube's puzzled head

Southern Cross (to Giuseppe Ungaretti)
On high the fables blaze

The aurora australis came and went
It was lost in the past
Ungaretti
You lasted

Wherever you are read now
a searchlight beacon reaches
into fog

Born in the shade of the beam of
the great lighthouse
of Alexandria
you knew the hard
Egyptian stars
twenty years
before you set foot
on the factual shore
of Italy
to begin
a pilgrimage
in silence
at night
in the dark
over mountains
deserts
fragmented bodies

On high the fables blaze
at the first hint of a breeze
they'll flutter to earth
with the leaves

but when the wind picks
up again
there will be a new star
in the southern sky

When you were old and silvery and raging
You wrote You were shattered

At eighty
you gave
Ed Sanders
one of your pubic hairs
to sell to speculators
to pay the costs
of his poetry magazine

At that same time
Ted Berrigan
was constructing an homage to you
deliberately mistranslated

Tootin' My Horn on Duty

Giuseppe
Your poetry burned out of your soul
by the suffering around you
in the most horrible of wars
remains as hard as bits of stars

When I think about you now

I always remember that
under the Southern Cross's wild conflagration
your father
helped build
the Suez Canal

"Who needs Apollo…" *(with Ted Berrigan)*

Money is boring
Who needs ideas

Who needs hot tears
Which drown ordinary joy

Who needs Apollo 15
Not me

I need the moon
To remain free

I want to go on
And to be on

A silver dollar
Still alive

I want to be on
My human feet

Spending my days
Like sunlight, opening

The people
And talking to them

What Is That Bright Star Next to the Moon Tonight?

Out late and looking again to the hazed red urban evening sky
    for a sign
What is that bright star next to the moon tonight?
Asking myself this among other questions of fleeting
    consequence
I watched Jupiter the great fluid king of the night
With his rude belching gases and submissive fluctuating moons

His swashbuckling bright streaks flaunted like sans culottes
Boiling firestorm spots and magnetic auroras
Cozying up, it seemed, to the chaste and shying
Waxing gibbous Lady Luna — seeming so close,
Though in reality far more distant and intense,

With nothing of her ethereal luminous
Silent running beauty, her unearthly milky violet glow —
Challenging her brightness perhaps
Though hardly her pulchritude —
Until my view grew occluded under the constellated neons

Of the Pyramid Ale House

Andromeda

Andromeda you give birth to new stars in your vast dusty arms
Swaths of red dust in wide lanes spin round
Twisting all the way into your center to be born
At your core smooth seas of older blue stars burn unregarding
At your heart crammed full of astral creation
Everything is dominated by starlight

De Ira Dei

Anger may be a necessary element in the character of God.

In fact given what is to be looked upon
In the mirror of an ever more exposed creation

With an eye that shines through the hole
In the ozone, clouded by thawing tears, perhaps

It is difficult *not* to make out iris and pupil in
The envelope of gas expelled by a dying star.

Anyone There?

In the end, the constellations emerge
Rich and bewildering in paratactic
Defiance of the night's strange high blankness—
But don't changes always illuminate that way,
A logic of radiance, no signs or sighs,
Only stony silences crossing lines with
The phone in eternity that rings and rings?

Crepuscular

Big clown-faced parallel infinity
you cried into my false twilight
a moon cupped in your creamwhite hands
poured milky awareness over me
more to feed my dream than to drown my fear

your tears blurry with repetitiveness
pearly sand grains scattered over that mandrake
root shaped cloud mass, opening into night
as if out through the motion space
of a two-way mirror, to where those planets

open into that lake

that ocean

White Moon

A noise would awaken or impersonate Kim.
As if these things were self evident
In her sleep ancient lunar fish enacted,
As if before an underwater window,
A comic mimicry of a sunken world,
The one Kim wished to inhabit — as if
Wishing were the next best thing to being
There. When the white moon comes up in the black
Cold winter night, the skin of empire drifts off
Like a poison that's evaporated;
Funny, thought Kim, how the film over words
Loses its toxic power in certain lights
Above implication's dowager kingdom.

Survey Research

Night, rain, lamps, man in the street—what does he want,
And that child he was, his mother wondering
As she stands holding his hand in the rain
What chance of happiness awaits him,
What happens now? I think a bus comes, the town
Simpleton plucks at the grass, all these silent
Faces fill the square, false moons in wet midnight—
The fleet probably already lost, yet no
Talk yet of wrecks of hats found floating,
The bandbox filling up with ghosts, the mothers
And wives who've been through all this before,
Who know the ships will be lost whispering
No warnings to the tiers of shadowy trees,
No rumours of life, no other signs so far.

Contraction

My heart, then, though small, was full — having caught
In summer through the fractured wall a glimpse
Of daylight, at the thought of where I was
I gladdened more than if I had beheld
Before me some bright cavern of Romance,
Or than we do, when on our beds we lie
At night, in warmth, when rains are beating hard,
The radio playing — a distant ballgame
In some city we've never seen, but dreamed,
And then, the rain driving through the night
Silences everything the passing years
Incorporate into their dying bodies,
The way stars dissolve, with long thinking,
Into the harrowed centres of themselves.

Glassitude

Silence is a distillate of noise.
Beneath the traffic hum and whoosh a tiny
Island of quiet is deposited
An oasis of reflection leached out
Of a symphony of power saws
The mechanical tools of human convenience.

Whereas:
In the universe of glass I dream
(Which is actually made of icy words)
The glass boat that floats in
A glass pool to the musical
Silence of a glass étude…
Is absolutely unheard.

Entertainment Medium

Flying through air, hanging upside down,
Tumbling, defying gravity for a lark:

Life going on while containing closure,
What in the world could be more common,

So, human; passing; thus, why requiring pain?
Loss sensed as hurt down through the drab ages;

Why not, one might ask, as freedom from same?
Forlorn the very word is like a bell

Miss Interpretation takes as an alarm
When may hap it might signal a homeward tolling;

Could also sound like a child's toy horn; to a clown
Tones of desolation might trigger laughter

Or tears; from the cheap seats all's equal either
Way; any sort of show brings down the house:

Flying through air, hanging upside down,
Tumbling, defying gravity for a lark.

The Self-Unseeing

His anxiety in the face of death
that walks hand in hand through the forest deep
with his anxiety in the face of life
standing beside the savage innocent
the innocuous mirage
the invincible ignorance of the boy
his own image in that burning pool
his penchant for destroying everything

Mnemonic

If on the moon palace stairs
A thin wash of water colour bleeding

Across the body chemistry frontier blurs,
As traffic slowly hones the blade of evening

And scatters its eyes across dusk's drift and growth,
That sharp outline we think of as reality,

It would perhaps be time to go to Plan B—
That is, to try to remember the colours of the morning.

Something in the Air: statement on the poems

The American poet/critic Bill Knott, speaking of Tom Clark's new work, has pointed to "the flow, the melodic momentum, the words in their intricate meaning(s), it's all done with such subtle touches, [the poet] in perfect control of his technique."

Clark writes of "how the film over words / Loses its toxic power in certain lights..." This new clearer, more candid illumination — from which "the skin of empire drifts off / Like a poison that's evaporated" — he would discover in the imagination of a pure poetic state of dream, reverie and play, emerging palpably out of the "slipstream blankness" of the empty canvas / page and out of the things of an immediate human and natural world.

A poet of original vision and gentle, careful word-shaping, Clark allows his images to merge and converge toward a resolution in which flow is not arrested but pauses to take thought; the images take over the controls and "do the talking," almost as if they had a mind of their own. What a relief when that happens, the poet confesses; he just follows along and tries to stay out of the way of whatever it is they seem to want to be saying.

And when the elements of image and sound and sense do then mysteriously come together in the moment, as Clark here proposes, "A point is fixed..."

Biographical note: Tom Clark

Tom Clark was born in Chicago in 1941 and educated at the University of Michigan, Cambridge University and the University of Essex. He has worked variously as an editor (*The Paris Review*), critic (*Los Angeles Times, San Francisco Chronicle, New York Times*) and biographer (lives of Damon Runyon, Jack Kerouac, Charles Olson, Robert Creeley, Edward Dorn), has written novels (*Who is Sylvia?, The Exile of Céline, The Spell*) and essays (*The Poetry Beat, Problems of Thought: Paradoxical Essays*). His many collections of poetry have included *Stones, Air, At Malibu, John's Heart, When Things Get Tough on Easy Street, Paradise Resisted, Disordered Ideas, Fractured Karma, Sleepwalker's Fate, Junkets on a Sad Planet: Scenes from the Life of John Keats, Like Real People, Empire of Skin, Light and Shade* and *The New World*. He lives in Berkeley, California with his wife and partner of forty-two years, Angelica Heinegg.

Poetry Books by Tom Clark

Stones (Harper & Row, 1969)

Air (Harper & Row, 1970)

Green (Black Sparrow, 1971)

Neil Young (Coach House, 1971)

John's Heart (Goliard/Grossman, 1972)

Smack (Black Sparrow, 1972)

Blue (Black Sparrow, 1974)

At Malibu (Kulchur, 1975)

When Things Get Tough on Easy Street: Selected Poems 1963–1978 (Black Sparrow, 1978)

A Short Guide to the High Plains (Cadmus, 1981)

Paradise Resisted: Selected Poems 1978–1984 (Black Sparrow, 1984)

Disordered Ideas (Black Sparrow, 1987)

Fractured Karma (Black Sparrow, 1990)

Sleepwalker's Fate: New and Selected Poems 1965–1991 (Black Sparrow, 1992)

Junkets on a Sad Planet: Scenes from the Life of John Keats (Black Sparrow, 1994)

Like Real People (Black Sparrow, 1995)

Empire of Skin (Black Sparrow, 1997)

White Thought (Hard Press/The Figures, 1997)

Cold Spring: A Diary (Skanky Possum, 2000)

Light and Shade: New and Selected Poems (Coffee House, 2006)

The New World (Libellum, 2009)

Trans/Versions (Libellum, 2009)

Something in the Air was designed by George Mattingly
in November 2009 using Neutraface Text fonts
based on signage design by architect Richard Neutra.

www.ingramcontent.com/pod-product-compliance
Lightning Source LLC
Chambersburg PA
CBHW031154160426
43193CB00008B/361